Inkblot and Altar

Inkblot and Altar

by
Laura Van Prooyen

Pecan Grove Press San Antonio, Texas

Cover design by Tim Clyne.

ISBN: 1-931247-37-4

Pecan Grove Press
Box AL
1 Camino Santa Maria
San Antonio, TX 78228

ACKNOWLEDGMENTS

I am grateful to the editors of the following publications where versions of these poems first appeared:

32 Poems Magazine—"Piñata"

After Hours: a journal of Chicago writing and art—"Three Encounters Not to be Ignored" and "What is it about the sizzle"

Another Chicago Magazine—"Sympathy for the Virgin"

Blackbird—"Males Often Have Brilliant Colors"

Christianity and Literature—"Israel"

Cimarron Review—"The space between"

Poetry Center of Chicago Big Table Chapbook—"He tried, but"

Poetry Motel—"Physics of You"

Rattle—"Convert's Lament"

Red River Review—"How to Kill the Romance," "The End of Any Affair," "Lenten Sestina," "The Mind Left to Its Own Devices" and "Morning Song"

Shades of December—"From a Train Window" and "Axis"

The Texas Observer—"Habits of Lovers and Bats"

Tiferet—"*Calvary* Is Not Far From *Cavalry*" and "Locusts and Honey"

Special thanks go to Jill Alexander Essbaum, Lynda Jordan, John Buri, and the ladies of Little Table, especially Joanne Diaz. Thanks also to H. Palmer Hall for publishing these poems. Finally, my deepest gratitude goes to my husband, Tim Clyne, and our girls.

*For Tim, who has been with me
from the beginning, is now, and ever shall be.*

CONTENTS

ON THE SHORELINE

Her vision is unreliable, as are her prayers.
She begs the lake to guide her, but expects nothing
more than this mantra of lapping. A boat
trolls by, the fishermen nearly indistinguishable
from trees. In this light, the great blue heron
on the dock could be anything: a child, or lovers
folding themselves into each other. It opens its wings;
the span is alarming. It beckons, urges her
to walk upon water. She offers her foot to the surface,
and for a moment, she believes it is possible.

HABITS OF LOVERS AND BATS

Their love is something remarkable
like Texas, bigger than she dare consider.
But its bridges are too near the water
to make jumping dramatic. So she won't.

And he won't. Though he hangs on
to the idea of her like a guardrail
where he lingers, poised above the river.

It is like this they go together
to watch the emergence of bats.

They cling to the underside of possibility.
As dusk approaches, so begins
the ritual of incredible flight.
A million wings extend
toward darkness; this great plume
trails away in last light.

THREE ENCOUNTERS NOT TO BE IGNORED

I.
This poem meets her on the porch
where it caught her sweeping leaves
from cobwebs, shaking out the rug
that welcomed it to the door.
It wants her in white cotton,
gowned like her mother or another
productive wife as she brooms clean
a fresh morning. No white gown
for her, but the sweeping she will do.
Dirt sifts down through cracks like flour
dusting the years stashed under
the stairs, the hiding place of children.

II.
A girl is prostrate under a table screaming
because her mother stirred the oatmeal
and poured the juice. The mother considers
the offending spoon and inconsolable daughter.
She sighs at another day's lesson of autonomy
and concludes: *I want no control*.

III.
And now she's found lingering on a corner
between the coffee shop and pub
where she once met her previous lover
who told her *you look ravishing*.
She recounted this to a friend,
but mistakenly said *ravenous*.
And still, she looks beautiful and hungry.

Morning Song

A train breaks the quiet
and whistles through my gown.
The neighbor's dog knows
the routine, doesn't bother barking.

The house lies still,
but the distant rumble is hypnotic:
listen, listen, listen.

A cricket upsets a leaf; a bird hesitates,
sings before light. The June bug
tortures the screen and my lashes
sweep the pillow in rhythm

with his sleep who will wake
after it's over,
just as the coffee is poured.

INKBLOT AND ALTAR

She must wash, always, both
hands. Saline dropped

into just one eye is never right.
It's like the Taj Mahal or maple

leaf. Spider web and starfish.
She believes in symmetry. Dragonfly.

Snowflake. An opened book.
Harmonious halves: W, X and Y.

She cannot let go of mountains
mirrored in the pond. Nevermind

the lopsided sag of her own down-
turned lip. Her librarian's lazy eye.

On the sidewalk a dog is dragging
its withered hind leg. The cathedral

has a chipped facade. Even Christ
she sees hanging, head drooped to one side.

SYMPATHY FOR THE VIRGIN

Imagine Mary's surprise when Jesus got colic.
One blessed, incessant screaming bundle
taking away the sin of the world.
Have mercy on us.

To whom does the Mother of God pray
when a pillow finds its way into her hands
lifted just above what is supposed to be
a cherub, a gift, salvation
and she looks again, hands shaking
but swears they are not hers.

The baby cried all day again.
At least if I screw up
I don't have a line of sinners
waiting in the hallway for redemption.

Yet, there is little comfort
in wishing away those tiny fingers
and resenting milk-filled breasts.

So one hand is in constant Rosary
while the other strokes circles

on the fragile back that rises and falls
in the same rhythm as prayer.

If only an angel would have come before this
to tell me it will all turn out all right.

A Muse, a Fluke and Displaced Affection

You showed up at my door
uninvited, again.

Did you misread this distant gaze?
I was searching, yes,
but for a different disaster.

There have been five fires
on this block since I moved in.
Everyone was rescued.

No one seems to question
the mystery of coincidence

unless you count me.

Which brings me back
to you, luckless chance.

We raffled in love's lottery
knowing all along we'd lose.

No, this musing will not do.
I implore the match
another strike.

This one is no accident.

I am pounding plywood
on the windows
while the core is still ablaze.

It is not safe.

WHAT IS IT ABOUT THE SIZZLE

in the pan, the oil that jumps
to sting the skin
the circle of heat
drawing me in *too close,*
too close.

There is no stepping
back. No turning
down the flame—
this flicker, this blaze.

I quit counting
as my days fell
fickle and thin.

But inside this rim
intensity sparks
your return:

our bristle, our burn.

PRAIRIE RESTORATION

I envy the torch and fire-
man, how he bends
to light tall grass; it catches
and snaps into quick
roiling blades.

How I do enjoy
the spectacle of flames,
though I'd be happier
with a sign.

A bush would be
fine, but God
already did that trick,
and this far-flung suburb
is short on wandering
rams. Too bad

the low moan I hear
is an airplane overhead.
The ash and blackened
scars, I see, are simply that.

My neighbor is waving
through the smoke,
calling my name. He
will not stop
until I wave back.

CONVERT'S LAMENT

Oh Joseph. I never had a question about you
getting some love. Mary either, for that matter. But now
I hear there's perpetual virginity, which might be just fine
for the Blessed Mother. She's been rewarded with altars,
statues, mudflaps and tattoos. But who's tattooing you?
There are few requests for Joseph the Celibate
to be needled on a bicep. The mythic allure
of an undefiled grown man just doesn't wash.
I'm wondering if, when the angel appeared, he laid
all your luck out on the table. You didn't seem to flinch
with the news, but did he mention Mary would be the lover
of no one and you'd get to bed down with prayer?
Sure, you're the honorary head of the Holy Family,
and I suspect you were loyal to the cause.
But after shaking off the glow of that angel,
and the white light began to fade
did you understand that Mary would remain
the foretaste of the feast that would never come?

You

are my loquat
silly fruit
jammed and jarred and spread—
right across my bread.

READY HARVEST

She with the peach. There is mischief
in the pit that broods within
this cloven fruit. It's easy
to mistake her for a simple
farm-stand yield. Her roadside life
invites the tourist and his boredom
to this landscape. A jackrabbit springs
from a hollow. The vendor lifts her skirt
full of peaches and releases them
to the bins. Her hands flit like monarchs
picking and packing wares into tightly-
woven baskets. She assembles a bright hill
and there, atop its peak, splits open
her most enticing halves.

FROM A TRAIN WINDOW

An omen puts her on a train to Budapest.
Her Libran stars balance the scales
to assure her; constellations do not lie.

There will be a sign. The city
will tell her why she does not love him,
but why she stays. Why, like some cancer
she eats herself away, in hopes of old
age and porch fronts. But this love
will not crochet and sip tea.
No, a seasoned life would be a gift.
She is less hopeful than a fossil
in a whirlpooling tide
left to erode, oh so slowly.

She wants to be this city:
her history unwoven for some new traveler.
She unfolds herself like a map for the loverless
lover, offers up her cobbled streets, opens
her museums, private collections, becomes
the Basilica, revels in longing.

The Mind Left to Its Own Devices

She fell like wet sand on the porch swing
dogs and babies strollered past her brazen, bare-faced
sleep. But she was busy meeting a man with a moustache
bobbing over the O of his mouth disclosing something vital,
but indiscernible. And quick as could be, he became a bear
with a piece of chalk. Holding her snug around the shoulders,
they drew lines connecting stars in night's sky: Big Dipper
Orion, and new constellations he designed. This until,
with another swift reversal, he was incarcerated in a tank top
and shoulder-to-wrist tattoos of blue flames and mermaids.
He had yet another moustache, suspicious thing, though his head
was extraordinarily bald. And he said, *It is strange to keep meeting
this way.* She turned on her smile and blushed without knowing why.

JUST LIKE A SUITCASE

She unpacks herself
in his room and bed
and mouth

which surrenders
no declaration apart from:
I have strong arms.

And she supposes he does.

But she can hardly snap shut
and be carried

when he does not understand
what he is holding.

RAVAGE IS NOT FAR FROM RAPTURE

Love, you are terrible
as an angler.
Just look at the errant
hook stuck in your brow.

Come now, try another cast.
How many times can your spinning
reel unspool?

Listen, I know a place
in dark water. You can troll
close to my shore; here,
throw out your lure.

Count me, then, among your catch
and splay me on the dock.

Is there any other way
but to take it quickly to the bone?
No, do not wait.
Bring my belly to the blade—
open me like wings.

WHITEOUT

This snow is a set of wings
come undone.

Or is it my heart
feathered and flaked
in suspended descent?

It's been coming down all day.

A restless sparrow,
wintering in my breast,
beats within this hollow—
the span of your love,
the size of your hand.

Take heart! (You did.)

Take flight, burdened wings
wet with this affliction
of want.

My world is disappearing
from the ground up.

White gone
white upon relentless
white covering my tracks.

Covering *this* and *that*—
the definition of our days,
your rake and my spade.

Our garden lost its shape.
The lamb's ears, first to go.
And now the earth itself
has gone cold, cold, cold.

I'm sickened
with the gentle slope.

This vanishing.

This wind that wings
your absence. The drift
against my fence—
a row of sharpened pickets
with barely a point left.

Together We Identify Few Birds

We know duck.

We saw a mother, once,
assail a descending seagull
(well, we also know *seagull*)
that was after the bread
thrown to her young.

Lucky we have the ducks.

Even those roasted
and plucked, hung
by necks in Chinatown
allow us to point, assured
we are right when
we name them: *duck*.

Otherwise, much eludes us.
We fail to make out
what stirs in the branches.
A flock of *something* blazes
across the sky. For all
we know, the birdsong
we whistle is a warning,
a call to take flight.

MALES OFTEN HAVE BRILLIANT COLORS

Let's begin with the escape. She is running
a good clip when in the street she is taken
by the surprise of his bright body.

He darts from curb to curb in the absence
of traffic. She sees, though distanced
and dragging, the eyes of
his magnificent plumes.

Let's begin again. The escape.
This week alone, there were eight.
The sheriff is embarrassed; the laundry
truck driver unnerved. But what effect

does this have on a tidy block
of bungalows, sidewalks chalked
with hopscotch. Or on the hedgerow

or boxcar concealing a man
who sniffs the air like a hound. What
does it mean to the man, himself,
who removes his shoes to feel again

the grass. Or to the woman
on the third floor watching
the news, plucking her brows
hoping for his call. What does it say

to the runner who happens
upon a peacock giving the slip
to the zoo, who does nothing but
moon over his feathers and crown.

Zoo

Habitually, Tuesday came and found the mother
strapping her daughters into carseats and heading
to the zoo. Since the mother quit questioning
what the second day of a work-week might offer, Tuesday
was quite happy to stake its claim. The zoo, too,
was content to expect the trio who always came
with mossy pellets for the goats.

What a surprise, then, the morning the mother blinked awake
and stretched her arms over her head, thinking
her body, at that moment, resembled a Y.
Hmmm, she thought, *I'm near the end of this alphabet.*

In this spirit, she took her girls to the zoo. The animals
were not sure how to behave. Turtles, for the first time,
stuck out their heads, lumbered toward water. Lemurs
jumped high in branches and, like streamers, hung down
black and white ringed tails. The kookaburra, that dull
gray nothing of a bird, burst out with the strangest
laughing cackle, a monkey's wild call.

Lenten Sestina

A craftsman vows to give up
the buzz of his saws and promises forty days
of rotating blades in silence. Without
sound he meditates on the way
he splinters the board and himself; the scent
of wood, a surprising delicacy that stirs

his thoughts to the woman who once stirred
in his bed. Surely, he thinks, she has given up
chocolate and is driven mad by its scent.
He recently stopped counting the days
since he'd seen her, but the way
she twisted hair around her finger leaves him without

defense. He knows why he must be without
her, but in this noiseless vacuum his head stirs
down the spiraling staircase to the way
her back arched when she lifted up
but not quite off—hours felt like days.
When she had to go, he would not shower her scent

off his skin. This love, this woman, had sent
prudence off packing; he was left simply without
judgment. He breaks with a cigarette, smokes in a daze,
wonders at how the wing of such a lovely bird stirs
the air, forever changing what has been known up
to this point. Self-inflicted penance of silence—a way

to make amends and discover the way
back to something divine. The fresh and earthy scent
of wood, he hopes, will conjure up
some vision of Christ. For years he has been without
much heavenly conviction, so he waits for something to stir
his spirit. The answer, he concedes, must be in these forty days.

His saws have been ordered quiet for less than a day,
but already his morning work has offered way
to small solace. He did not consider, however, that stirring
his coffee would clink the spoon or the scent
of rich cream would leave him without
remorse, make him lift his eyes up,

but stir his spirit further from the cross and send
him longing for past days, asking no forgiveness for the way
he lived without conscience and loved until his strength
        was used up.

HE TRIED, BUT

what sounds clever in bed
cannot sit comfortably on a park bench at noon.

LOCUSTS AND HONEY

Cicadas cracked their shells seven years early.
They litter sidewalks, tree trunks; delicate leaves
hang heavy with discarded nymphs.

She wonders what this has to do with her
own calamity. A desire older than Moses
plagues her. Her heart,
stubborn as a Pharaoh, stands
with a bullwhip at the back of yearning,
but will not let it go. Neither
hail nor darkness can persuade her.
And now the locusts have come.

She does not heed warning. She turns,
instead, into the desert stretched out
for a holy wanderer. He preaches his way
into this river. It is there he will baptize,
there consume wild honey.

THE WHEEL

The mother suddenly finds herself afraid. For years
she has been atop skyscrapers, forehead to the glass,
marveling over the cool grid of the world. But when
she takes her daughters on the Ferris wheel,
it is the fresh air that terrifies. She considers her girls
and pinches a smile, though her hope for a new
horizon rocks on the rickety cart that cautions:
this could be the end, and you're not ready.
She tries to comfort herself with a focal point,
but can only manage to see the shifting clouds.
Her daredevil baby stands on the benchseat. The sister,
suspecting something awry, points to the treetops
and wishes the trio were birds. The mother clings
to her daughter's shoulder as if it could save her.
As if that's what the child was sent there to do.

First Miracle

Water to wine would be amazing enough.

If that's what this was about.

Consider Mary
urging her unwilling Jesus,
in spite of what she knew would come of it.

And how mothers—
before and since—
discover rows of jars,
suspect their emptiness,

and know they must send
their children away
to fill them.

Mosaic

His walking away
has become a ritual.

Waiting for the turnaround,
she aches like broken pottery.

S. O. S.

She took the chestnut tree as her lover.
A jealous maple rooted itself in the parkway,
but the chestnut offered bunches
of big leaves that seemed exotic
from an undiscovered, tropical place.
So she sat in the branches stroking the bark
and devised a plan of survival
in case she found herself on an island
about to be deserted.

EXILE

Moses, my Moses,
stand on this hill and be damned
if I am not *your* promised land.

You've been wandering too long
and I lie here outstretched, outpoured.

God's got a grudge, dear boy.
He has not forgotten the way we came
together, my rock smitten by your rod.
Water flowed freely and yes,
it tasted good.

Alas, this vengeful God
cares little for us
or our longing.

Beloved Moses, if only we
could return to the sea
where for you, my waters parted.

Physics of You

My resistance equals the mass
of this matter—
not the weight—
because it depends on gravity
and the impact of words.

All that would change in outer space.

My bucket is upside down,
but the water will not spill out.
This is the part of the universe
that does not rely on emotion.

The string of our centripetal force
has been broken. We're thrown
into constant velocity;

we carry on without formula,
no predictable outcome
or external net force
to stop us.

THE SPACE BETWEEN

Texarkana and El Paso. Lines
on the road. Telephone poles. The space
between my arrival and your departure.
Your upper and lower lip. This cigarette
and my next drag. The space
between headboard and footboard. Sheet
and skin. Sigh and sleep. A ring
and its finger. Dialtone
and your answer.
My foot and the brake.
The bridge and river.
Your last kiss and this:

HOW TO KILL THE ROMANCE

Suicide would be a gift to this love.
The poem suggests a gun.
The television has seen a good episode with pills.
The warden recommends a shoestring noose
to dispose of unrestrained and troublesome affairs.
The grandmother offers her recipe for oleander tea,
while the hairdryer looks longingly at the full tub.
The lover conspires with a tailpipe,
but has no access to the ignition, let alone keys.
In spite of all the helpful advice, this little darling carries on.

The End of Any Affair

I see, he said, and then an old woman
across the street opened her car door
and thrust out one heavy sole
at a time. Legs planted like momentary oaks,
she pulled her wool cap to kiss her eyebrows
and clutched the collars of her coat
in defense, or maybe surprise.

GETHSEMANE

How shall I tend this withered vine?
The olive blossoms have expired.
The garden is stripped, my palms
are pricked by stubborn thorns.

Passion often grows like this:
with suffering (a curious thing)
if I bear it well, I'm soothed.
Precisely why I suffer so.

This my sorrowful mystery:
I'm faithful to love's dying plot.
The season of our bounty gone.
My heart, a spade of fresh-turned earth.

Axis

If I were only so content
with your routine:

a shave, the newspaper,
and the fact that
tomorrow will arrive
just the same.

Despite my attempts
the century turns

in seconds, pouring out
fast, like milk; cereal rises
in the bowl.

The habit of the sun
is appalling. Morning light.
Pane shadows stretching,
consistent. Method

without apology: always.

CALVARY IS NOT FAR FROM CAVALRY

Either way, she has her doubts
about rescue.
She comes to this graveyard
in search of a Christ. It would be nice
to whisk him free of dust and let herself
unroll. Spread clean the white of her page
and tape the edges down.

She'd like to stroke the crayon and coax
the coming of a new messiah, who might emerge
a man she'd fold and take home.

Her redeemer, though, may not be so easy
to preserve. This is not the first time
a whole night of rubbing
found her at daybreak
empty-handed, empty-hearted, still.

PIÑATA

Something happened to the mother while serving cake.
The piece that was to be hers, she gave away.
Then there was nothing left to do but line the children up.

The baby began with harmless tapping.
But with each child's turn the beating
gained momentum.

A single blow tore off an ear. Then went the legs.
Soon after, the blue burro was split
through its hollow breast.

Candy flew down like hail.
The children
stuffed their mouths and bags and took
all there was to be taken.

In the morning, a sparrow hopped across the lawn,
shreds of the burro in her beak.

Song

This morning doves
are mourning—
their resounding
coo coo coo
sounds like *you*.

CREDENCE

This town is not mine.
It's yours and yours.

It belongs to the phone booth
that took my tired change.

It belongs to the breakwater
cradling the shore, and the stranger
beside me who lets himself see
smokestacks in Gary
but calls them Chicago.
I almost correct him:
You're wrong!   You're wrong!

He wants to believe
the one he believes in,
so it must be right.

AFTEREFFECT

As if absence was ever ours
to simply choose
like color for a wall.

We are long past deciding
whether this room feels
warmer in yellow. See,

here it is again,
your apparition
coming down my stairs.

This is not clear?

Look more closely. True,
the light is dim.

Listen how the footfalls
know their way.

We are not dead.
I don't believe in ghosts.

But I cannot deny,
the steam
in my shower
speaks.

My skin is tricked
into the presence
of your hand.

So That We May Feast

Our bodies fail us
so many ways it will
be a pleasure to leave.
But having said more
than one goodbye
I wish for each
her own (or his)
assumption—
tethered, please, not
to some undying
disease—so
loves and lovers
might always go on
with the possibility
of return.

Uses for Salt

Paul to the Colossians: *season your conversations.*

It's effective in an old adage about worthiness.

Some recited prayer. Others painted themselves,
danced, fasted and coiled snakes on their heads, even
invited them into their mouths. Little did they know
about weather modification and the seeding of clouds.

The perfect dressing for a margarita.

Think winter. Chicago. Ice.

A warning: run as fast as you can
and never look back. Follow the angels
who lead you from your Gomorrah,
without question. Accept God's mercy
lest you hope to become an unfortunate pillar
left for some wild animal to lick.

Resolution

The last of your
hair is
brushed
off my
pillow.
My sheet
on the line
is your deletion.

ISRAEL

Try as I might to find a sign, this cloud is just a cloud.
And the man approaching is simply the neighbor
with the mail, though I hoped for a burly wrestler
masquerading as the Lord himself with an offer
to bout for absolution. In fact, I've got my kneepads on,
my mouth guard in, hands bare, but open. I'm ready
for the takedown, the holy dislocation of my hip.
Pin me to the mat of forgiveness, let me
hobble away with a blessing and new name.

SERENITY PRAYER

Can there be a day more honest
than this that finds a mother
with her six children on a log
nestled in thick Wisconsin woods
reaching inside a beetle-blue
insulated sack for bologna
sandwich after sandwich with mayo
and mustard on white bread?
Seven full mouths, for a moment, quiet
while a deer, expectant of nothing,
steps into a ray of nearby sun.

Very Good Friday

The believers line up
to give the cross
a kiss. I kneel and wonder
if I missed the point of this
ritual. Women stroke
the wood as if it were
still warm; a boy rolls
his eyes at genuflecting
mourners unable to rise.

The faithful turn
to leave. I search
each face and want
to believe we are one.

But when the pews clear,
I'm fixed with doubt
and this faint prayer:
*Where to begin
but the beginning?*

First the darkness, then
the light. He, creator

of my heart. He who
spares no mystery:

*Forgive me Forgive
meForgiveme*

CHRIST, I ADORE YOU

You hate it when I call you Christ-
     like hate it from the bottom
     of your well-
spring soul, from the cockles
of your blessed heart
to tips of bloodied toes.

What else can I call you
who suffered this my Judas kiss
     (remiss! remiss!)
and in three days three hours three minutes
reassured, erected, resurrected
     reconciled all I wrecked.

So my Lord, my saving grace
cherub faced, crown of thorns
lifter of my secrets' shroud
roller of my graveyard stones:

I never meant to break your bones.
Sacrificial lamb, my Great I am
     I am
     mere bread
you are my life
you my water, I your wife
I drink to you, my potent wine
Christ, I adore you.
Christ, you're mine.

Recent Books from Pecan Grove Press

Barker, Wendy. *Between Frames*. 2006.
    ISBN: 1-931247-35-8 $9
Byers, Cluster R. *Revisions of Visions*. 2005.
    ISBN: 1-877603-81-3 $12
Challender, Craig. *Dancing on Water*. 2005.
    ISBN: 1-931247-20-x $12
Emmons, Jeanne. *Baseball Nights and DDT*. 2005.
    ISBN: 1-931247-26-9 $12.50
Essbaum, Jill Alexander. Oh Forbidden. 2005.
    ISBN: 1-931247-29-3 $9
Fargnoli, Patricia. *Small Songs of Pain*. 2004.
    ISBN: 1-931247-17-x $10
Gutierrez, Cesar. *Lonesome Pine*. 2006.
    ISBN: 1-931247-31-5 $9
Haddad, Marian. *Somewhere Between Mexico and a River Called
    Home*. 2004. ISBN: 1-931247-18-8 $15
Hochman, Will. *Freer*. 2006.
    ISBN: 1-931247-34-x $15
Hughes, Glenn. *Sleeping at the Open Window*. 2005.
    ISBN: 1-931247-25-0 $8
Hunley, Tom C. *My Life as a Minor Character*. 2005.
    ISBN: 1-931247-27-7 $8
Kasper, Catherine. *A Gradual Disappearance of Insects*. 2005.
    ISBN: 1-931247-22-6 $8
Kirkpatrick, Kathryn. *Beyond Reason*. 2004.
    ISBN: 1-931247-09-9 $12
McCann, Janet. *Emily's Dress*. 2004.
    ISBN: 1-931247-21-8 $8
Mankiewicz, Angela Consolo. *An Eye*. 2006.
    ISBN: 1-931247-33-1 $9
Pedraza, Venetia June. *Porcelain Dolls Break*. 2004.
    ISBN: 1-931247-19-6 $7

For a complete listing of Pecan Grove Press books and chapbooks from 1987-2006, please visit our web site:

http://library.stmarytx.edu/pgpress